Maryland's

EASTERN SHORE

A PHOTOGRAPHIC PORTRAIT

First published in the United States
of America by:

Twin Lights Publishers, Inc.
10 Hale Street
Rockport, Massachusetts 01966
Telephone: (978) 546-7398
http://www.twinlightspub.com

and

Yourtown Books
292 14th Avenue, Suite C
Naples, Florida 34102
Telephone: (941) 262-0716

ISBN 1-885435-33-9

10 9 8 7 6 5 4 3 2 1

Book design by
SYP Design & Production, Inc.
http://www.sypdesign.com

Cover Photo by: Charles Prahl
Back Cover Photos by: D. Graham Slaughter,
Joanne C. Gadomski, and Alan C. Dickerson

Printed in China

Contents

Maryland's Eastern Shore is a stretch of the Delmarva Peninsula over 100 miles long and almost 70 miles across at its widest point. Water is everywhere. With Chesapeake Bay on one side, the Atlantic Ocean on the other, and a myriad of rivers, creeks and inlets running through, it is interlaced with water—there are thousands of miles of shoreline.

The area's nine counties have the lowest population density in the coastal region from Norfolk to Portland. The beauty, variety and special appeal of the region lie in the unique blend of rural land, small town living, and waterfront access for all.

Locals, who enjoy natural beauty and a pace of life that runs with the tides and four distinct seasons, treasure the shore for what it lacks—gridlock, sprawl, and stress. Visitors from the surrounding Richmond to Philadelphia megalopolis find it a precious resource, a haven for renewal within driving distance.

Rivers bear the names of Native Americans who lived here for thousands of years before the English colonists. Tribes like the Nanticoke, Choptank and Assateague fished, hunted and grew corn, peas, squash and tobacco for trade. Captain John Smith is famous for his 1608 description of the "delightsome land," claiming that there is "no place more perfect for man's habitation."

For the history and preservation minded, there is a trove of landmark buildings, churches and historic sites. The arts are alive and well in museums and theaters throughout the region. Small towns create a sense of genuine community that has never been lost. People know each other by name. Just below the Mason-Dixon line, this is the place where the best of northern and southern culture are enjoyed.

The delicate interrelationship of farmland and estuary requires good environmental stewardship, and there are scores of exceptional wildlife preserves to visit. Many visitors fly to the area — geese, ducks and tundra swan. Abundant fresh seafood earned the shore its catchphrase, "the land of pleasant living." A broad consortium of experts is collaborating to replenish fisheries to historic levels for the health of the Bay and the sustenance of its residents.

The Chesapeake Bay provides some with a living and others with recreation. Boats are as low key as a dinghy or as high performance as a Donzi. Historic skipjacks commingle with crab boats, power yachts and freighters. Racing occurs in everything from cardboard boats to majestic log canoes. The Chesapeake Bay Maritime Museum in St. Michaels is an excellent place to learn about the diversity of craft.

Photographers have recorded their impressions of the upper, mid and lower reaches of the shore. Each region has a distinct character, but all share incredible diversity in landscape and activities. If you visit the area, we hope you'll see it all. If you live here, we anticipate that some of these photographs will cause you to look at your surroundings with new eyes or prompt you to take a back road that you haven't explored.

Maryland 1895

Judges' Background:

David Bishop

President, Hobby Horse, Inc. and Competition Photos, Inc
Easton, MD
www.hobby-horse.com

Dave Bishop is a professional photographer who operates the only serious camera shop on the upper or mid shore. He took over the reins of The Hobby Horse—his family's business—in 1977. A member of Professional Photographers of America, he has extensive wedding, special occasion and studio experience spanning more than 30 years. His real love is action—since 1966, his auto racing and hot rod photographs have appeared in USA Today and in 13 national racing magazines. Dave has judged numerous photographic works competitively in his career. We were fortunate to have his experienced eye and sense of location for the difficult task of selecting the top three from hundreds of quality works. We are grateful to him for his fine courtesy photographs of local landmarks. The Hobby Horse was helpful in promoting the contest and in providing technical support for the judging.

James D. Plumb

We were very fortunate to have a fine artist of Jim Plumb's caliber to judge these works. Jim is the Associate Professor of Art at Chesapeake College, where he teaches both the studio and art history courses. A past curator of the Academy of Arts in Easton, he holds an MFA from Brooklyn College where he studied under Lennart Anderson and Philip Perlstein. He was one of 20 students worldwide admitted to postgraduate studies at Masstricht Summer University in 2001. Jim has entered his earlier Photo-realist paintings and his portrait and still life work in numerous juried shows and has taken part in many invitational exhibitions. His work has won awards from directors and curators at the National Gallery, the Baltimore Museum of Art, the Hirshorn Museum, and New York's O.K. Harris Gallery. One of his drawings was selected for a touring show of Maryland artists, curated by Lee Fleming of Art News presented by Maryland Arts Place. In the past four years, he has taken two "Best of Show" awards and two "Juror's Choice" awards at Easton's Academy Art Museum. We are honored to have such a highly accomplished artist participate in the selection of our prizewinners.

David H. Stevens

www.horizonphotography.com

David has lived on the Eastern Shore for over 20 years, where he has worked in stained glass and wood sculpture, creating both public and private commissions. In addition to degrees in History and Elementary Education, he studied photography for several years in the late 1970's, and has been taking pictures all the while. His art has evolved to a point of full time self-employement as a photographer since 1999. He is represented in galleries in Easton, St. Michaels and Annapolis and through art festivals such as Sugarloaf's Arts and Crafts show. He has done freelance work for Chesapeake Bay Magazine and Spokes magazine. David brought the sensibilities of both a fine artist and a commercial photographer to the judging. We are grateful to him for several fine courtesy photographs as well.

Other Acknowledgements

Christopher J. Brownawell, Director, Academy Art Museum for hosting the judging at the museum.

www.art-academy.org

Hunter H. Harris
Fly Aloft Photography
www.fly-aloft.com

Hunter is a native (seventh generation) of the Eastern Shore, raised in Kent County on Bloomingneck Farm at the headwaters of the Chesapeake Bay. His 27 years of flying airplanes, seaplanes, helicopters, and gliders includes a proud nine-year career as an Airship (blimp) pilot. Now a resident of Talbot County, Hunter spends most of his time concentrating on his aviation pursuits, including aerial photography through his company, Aloft, Inc. We are grateful to Hunter for the countless hours he put into helping select the right mix of aerial perspectives from his collection of hundreds of photos. We also value his exciting courtesy shots.

Richard Ford

Richard Ford is a native of Upper Fairmount in Somerset County. He flew for the U.S. Coast Guard at Chincoteague, where he would familiarize new recruits with the area he knows so well. From his own planes, he has taken aerial photographs of the Eastern Shore since 1950. His rich archive documents the changes—and some of the lack of change—of the area. When he isn't flying, Dick keeps busy logging over 20,000 miles a year on his motorcycle. We are grateful for his illustrative lower shore aerials.

John T. Sener, contest coordinator

John T. Sener, ("Tenny"), has lived on the shore since 1966. He studied photography at the Maryland Institute in the early 1970's and has been an avid hobbyist ever since. John is a custom woodworker specializing in one-of-a-kind architectural pieces.

Priscilla Morris, captions

Priscilla Morris's ancestors were among the earliest settlers in Talbot County. She founded the Railway Market in Easton in 1979, and currently works as a business consultant.

Stuart Johnson, for his tireless enthusiasm and support for the project.

Sara Day, book design

Sara Day of SYP Design & Production, Inc. for the design and layout of this beautiful book.

Crab Caught Trot Lining

CHARLES PRAHL
CONTAX ST
KODACHROME 200
1/125

A trot liner on the Honga River caught this Maryland blue crab and an unsuspecting sea nettle, but it is Chuck Prahl who caught the real prize when he made this beautiful and provocative shot showcasing the Eastern Shore's favorite crustacean in the best possible light.

A Maryland native, Chuck has spent 25 years on the back roads and waters of the Chesapeake photographing the people, the vessels, and the myriad creatures of the area. He was looking for a creative outlet following a hunting accident, which left him paralyzed and confined to a wheelchair as a teenager. When his cousin sold him his camera, his photographic documentation of bay life began. His focus on Chesapeake Bay life encompasses the men and women who work on and beside "this magnificent watershed."

Chuck has a website at
www.chesapeakelife.com

Ready, Set, Go

MARY HITCHENS
CANON EOS ELANII
KODAK PORTRA NC
F-8

Steamers in operation at the Tuckahoe Steam and Gas Show in Talbot County north of Easton. The antique equipment that powered industry and agriculture on the Eastern Shore is preserved for all to see at the annual show the weekend after July 4th. Mary Hitchens recalled visiting the show as a child with her parents and when she returned recently with her husband Pete, she revisited those youthful memories as she recorded the goings on.

Mary is a medical assistant with a part time career as a professional photographer, which she calls "an answer to prayer." She finds expressing herself through photography "wonderfully rewarding." While claiming to be dissatisfied with her ability to express herself verbally, she creates evocative moods that speak volumes using her camera. Mary and her husband Pete live in Harrington, Delaware. Her part time profession is "Capture A Moment" Photography.

Great Blue Heron

NORMAN C. DULAK
NIKON D1
DIGITAL ISO 400
F-5.6

Norm Dulak's lifelong interest in wildlife has developed into a serious pursuit of wildlife photography in retirement. He holds a Ph.D. in Physiological Chemistry as well as a J.D. from the Fordham University School of Law. He brings the same depth and breadth of focus to his new endeavor as he did to his careers in academia and patent law.

From his home on the banks of Fairlee Creek, he tells us, "I can think of few other places where one, from the comfort of his living room, can observe dozens of blue herons in May or hundreds of tundra swans in February."

Upper Shore

CECIL, KENT, AND QUEEN ANNE'S COUNTIES

Turkey Point
Lighthouse *(previous page)*

HUNTER H. HARRIS
ALOFT AERIAL PHOTOGRAPHY
CANON EOS 1-N
FUJI 200
5.6/650/SEC.

From the high promontory at the
head of the Bay, lighthouse keepers
kept their aid to mariners lit from
1833 to 2000. Over the years,
four women kept the lighthouse
including Fanny Salter, who retired
in 1947.

◁ Father of Our Country

CHRISTINA N. GRANBERG
CANON EOS REBEL XS
KODAK GOLD 400
F-5.6

George Washington was honored
to give his name to the "college at
Chester." He also gave generously
of his time, money (50 guineas) and
educational vision to the first college
of the new nation. The founding of
Washington College in 1782 is
another important chapter in
Chestertown's rich colonial history.

△ St. Luke's Episcopal Church

ROBERT AUSTIN WALMSLEY
NIKON FM
FUJICHROME
F.16

Built c.1732 at Church Hill of handsome Flemish bonded brick; St.
Luke's features a lovely gambrel
roof and semi-circular apse. The
original construction was funded by
140,000 pounds of tobacco, the
currency of the time.

Customs House from
the Chester

ROBERT AUSTIN WALMSLEY
NIKON FM
KODACHROME

Legend has it that customs collector
William Geddes watched the original Chestertown Tea Party take
place on his brig from this building.
Built at the foot of High Street circa
1745, it is the largest surviving
Custom House of the 13 colonies.

△ To Market, To Market

HEATHER BROWN
FUJI
800 SPEED

The crew of the *Annie J* from Rock Hall weighs up the catfish on their way to market. Catfish like the brackish waters of the Upper Bay and can be found in the upper reaches of most rivers. They are fished both commercially and recreationally.

▷ Joie de Vivre

VIRGINIA BREUNINGER
OLYMPUS INFINITY
KODAK 400

Whether you live here or come "down" to the shore from the city on weekends, nothing beats the simple pleasure of speeding along with the wind in your hair.

◁ **Reflection** (top)

BARBARA O'CONNER
PENTAX
200

Mirror flat stillness on a calm cove
near Grasonville provides a pensive
moment for a mute swan. Mutes
are one of 7 species of swan—the
largest and most beautiful of
waterfowl with up to 25,000 feath-
ers in their entirely white plumage.

◁ **Breakfast is Served** (bottom)

NORMAN C. DULAK
NIKON D1
DIGITAL ISO 400
F-5.6

Osprey nests are a common sight
atop channel markers throughout
the Bay. Today's special is sashimi.

△ **Gentle Tide**

STACEY EMBERT
OLYMPUS
KONICA

Diversity makes for the beauty of
the Bay—from the quiet hidden
coves to the broad water and
sandy beaches. Here a sandy bend
stretches out from Terrapin Park
on Kent Island.

△ Chesapeake Classic

CHARLES PRAHL
CONTAX ST
KODACHROME 64
1/250

A skipjack slips by the Bay Bridge in the blue haze of late summer. The last of the working sailboats, some skipjack captains offer excursion sails to supplement the upkeep of

▷ Sultana

COURTESY OF
DAVID H. STEVENS
CANON EOS
KODACHROME
F-8

A replica of a tea tax collector, built 1999–2001. She was launched in time for the Chestertown Tea Party reenactment in spring, 2001.

The Amistad Visits the Chesapeake

ALLISON MORRIS
CANON A-1
FUJI 100
F-16 @1/125

A replica of the famous slave trader, Amsitad was launched on March 25, 2000. Now an educational ambassador, her mission reminds all races to stand united. She passes under the twin spans of the Chesapeake Bay Bridge heading to other ports to spread her message of freedom.

Trooping the Colors

RICHARD TAYLOR BAILEY
FUJI DISCOVERY 312
FUJI 400
AUTO/FLASH

In May of 1774, after the British closed the port of Boston in reaction to the Boston Tea Party, the irate citizens of Chestertown held their own tea party, boarding the British Brigantine "Geddes" and consigning its tea to the Chester River. A pre-Memorial Day parade and reenactment of the event takes place every year.

Chester River at Chestertown

ROBERT AUSTIN WALMSLEY
NIKON FM
KODACHROME
F-16

In view are Skipjack "Ellsworth" by
the dock, a bateaux by the fish net,
and the Old Wharf restaurant.

Tranquil Harbor

GEORGE W. SCHULTZ
NIKON
135
AUTO

The fleet's in and the sails are down.
Now is the perfect time to enjoy the
view from one of Rock Hall's many
fabulous seafood eateries.

It Was THIS Big!

ALLISON MORRIS
CANON A-1
FUJI 100
F-16 @1/60

A triumphant fisherman shows off his pumpkinseed or "sunny" from a dock on Southeast Creek.

Dawn's Early Light

RICHARD TAYLOR BAILEY
FUJI DISCOVERY 312
FUJI 400
AUTO/FLASH

Retrievers are excellent water dogs—hard working and extremely
loyal. Whether they are birding or just shaking creek water all over
the guests, they are part and parcel of tidewater living.

▽ Tranquil Lankford Bay

HUNTER H. HARRIS
ALOFT AERIAL PHOTOGRAPHY
CANON EOS 1-N
FUJI 200
5.6/650/SEC.

Nestled between Chestertown and Eastern Neck off the Chester
River, it is hard to believe this peaceful scene lies only 30 miles
from Baltimore or Annapolis as the crow flies!

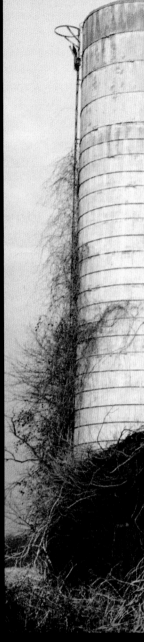

◁ **After the Harvest**

RICHARD TAYLOR BAILEY
FUJI DISCOVERY 312
FUJI 400
AUTO/FLASH

An evocative Quaker Neck farmscape at sunrise. Although not entirely immune to sprawl, Maryland's Eastern Shore still boasts many family farms preserving American traditions and wildlife habitat.

△ **Seasoned**

MARY BRYAN
RICOH 35
KODAK GOLD ASA 400

A stately gambrel roofed barn and silo near Church Hill remind us of the vital role of family farming in the Eastern Shore way of life.

Tropical Optical

STACEY EMBERT
OLYMPUS
KONICA

The right light and foliage create
an island mood at Terrapin Park
on Kent Island.

Interstate Flyway

ROBERT F. O'BRIEN
OLYMPUS
25 SP KODACHROME
F-1.6

Red skies illuminate an October sunset at Eastern Neck Wildlife Refuge.
With 2,285 acres where the Chester
meets the Bay, it is a major destina-
tion for thousands of migratory birds.

Friends of the Field

NORMAN C. DULAK
NIKON D1
DIGITAL ISO 400
F-5.6

A rare albino deer and a yearling spend a
poignant moment together. The burgeoning
deer population almost guarantees a native
white-tailed deer sighting where the fields
meet the woodland.

△ **Crumpton Bridge** *(top)*

JAMES R. DURHAM III
NIKON
35 MM

In colonial times, the rivers were the inter-state highways of the area. Now the roads make use of countless bridges to move travelers through the region. Local jazz pianist Dick Durham took a moment away from his keyboard to record two generations of high-ways on the way to Crumpton, population 689. Crumpton is famous for its antique auction held each Wednesday at Dixon's Furniture Sales.

△ **Upper Bay** *(bottom)*

HUNTER H. HARRIS
ALOFT AERIAL PHOTOGRAPHY
CANON EOS 1-N
FUJI 200
5.6/650/SEC.

A tanker heads for the C and D canal on the Upper Bay at Betterton. Betterton Beach, being in the less salty upper reaches of the estuary, is a great place to swim free of late summer's stinging sea nettles.

Mid Shore

CAROLINE, TALBOT, AND DORCHESTER COUNTIES

Inn at Perry Cabin (previous page)

HUNTER H. HARRIS
ALOFT AERIAL PHOTOGRAPHY
NIKON 8008
FUJI 200
8/1000/SEC.

Perry Cabin was built just after the War of 1812 near "the town that fooled the British" by Samuel Hambleton, aide-de-camp to Commodore Oliver Hazard Perry. Known for its fine Eastern Shore accommodations for many years, it was converted to a world-class luxury inn by Sir Bernard Ashley. He appointed it in the English country manor style of his late wife, Laura Ashley. Now operated by Orient-Express Hotels, it has been named one of the top 12 inns in the US by *Country Inns* magazine.

△ Fresh Perspective

HUNTER H. HARRIS
ALOFT AERIAL PHOTOGRAPHY
NIKON 8008
FUJI 200
8/1000/SEC.

Given the history and difficulty of log canoe racing, the sport is well documented. Hunter Harris adds to the record by focusing directly down into the racing, affording us a glimpse of the drama at the helm and a taste of the spectacular thrill of riding the outriggers.

▷ Sailor's Delight

MARY HITCHENS
CANON EOS ELANII
KODAK PORTRA NC
F-16

"Red skies at night, sailor's delight. Red skies at morn, sailors take warn."

If there's any truth to the ditty, this boat heading into Oxford will have fabulous sailing tomorrow.

Creature from Below

D. GRAHAM SLAUGHTER
HASSABLAD
PRO COLOR
F-11

A marine dwelling animal has left
it's tracks in the sediment of a
Blackwater marshscape.

Full House

D. GRAHAM SLAUGHTER
F5 NIKON
NPS
F-5.6

Osprey perch on their nest at sunset.

ESTHER F

◁ **"Drudgin" Oysters**

COURTESY OF
DAVID H. STEVENS
CANON EOS
TMAX 100
F-8

△ **Skipjack Bowsprits**

COURTESY OF
DAVID H. STEVENS
CANON EOS
TMAX 100
F-22

Under sail, watermen have dredged oysters from the bottom of the Bay since the 19th century. Now Maryland's State Boat, skipjacks are the last commercial workboats under sail in the country. The fleet has diminished to very few working boats and even those have to rely on the tourist trade to make ends meet.

The early morning fog rises on Dogwood Harbor at Tilghman Island. Sails are ready to hoist at the first breath of air.

Sunrise Over the Creek

STUART M. JOHNSON
NIKON N 60
KODAK GOLD 200
F-8

Stuart says that this shot most rep-
resents the area for him. As the
earliest bird takes flight and the
mist rises from the creek, there is a
brief moment of intense color and
serenity before the composure of
the empty docks is replaced with
the daily bustle.

Lightkeeper's Changes

JOYCE PHILLIPS
FUJI DISCOVERY 1000
KODAK GOLD 2000
AUTO

Sunrise begins to take over the duties at Hooper Strait lighthouse, now on the grounds of the Chesapeake Bay Maritime Museum. Originally two men stood watch all night to keep the oil light lit and to ring the bell in fog. This type of lighthouse was built over the water on pilings.

Off To The Races

MICHAEL J. KABLER
CANON A-1
FUJI -100
F-8 @ 1/60

Triton 28 *Inka* heads up the Miles River for the Wednesday Night Races near St. Michaels. Wednesday night racing occurs all over the bay with boats of all sizes and rigs participating at varying levels of handicap.

△ **So Proudly We Hail**

GLORIA FAULKNER
NIKON N 70
KODAK
F-4

Fireworks at St. Michaels are viewed from land and
sea. In 1813 the town fooled the British into over-
shooting the town by staging a blackout and hanging
lanterns from the tops of masts and trees. A year later
at Baltimore harbor, Frances Scott Key penned the Star
Spangled banner after watching the British bombard-
ment of Fort McHenry.

▷ **Sultana at the Maritime Museum**

MICHAEL J. KABLER
CANON A-1
FUJI -100
F-11 @ 1/120

Two organizations join at the dock to fulfill their educational missions. The British flag serves as a reminder
of the original Sultana's use as a tea tax collector. She
patrolled the East Coast from Halifax to Chesapeake
Bay during the early revolutionary years. The British
Navy had meticulously documented her original lines,
enabling construction of an unusually accurate replica

△ Log Canoe Racing

COURTESY OF
HUNTER H. HARRIS
CANON EOS 1-N
KODAK T-MAX
5.6/650/SEC.

Chesapeake Bay log canoe racing dates back to the 19th century. #20 is the Edmee S., raced by John Valliant, President of the Chesapeake Bay Maritime Museum. Log canoe races are held at Chestertown, Rock Hall, St. Michaels, Oxford and Cambridge with the Miles River being the center of activity.

△ Small Town Nightlife

STUART M. JOHNSON
NIKON F 100
KODAK GOLD 100
F-22

Antiques, high-end specialties, and fine dining have re-energized Harrison Street and other blocks of downtown Easton in the environs of the Avalon Theater and the Academy Art Museum.

▷ Heading Home

MARY HITCHENS
CANON EOS ELANII
KODAK PORTRA NC
F-16

A couple of boaters on the Tred Avon take their sunset from the bow.

The Strand

COURTESY OF
DAVID BISHOP
NIKON N 90-S
KODACHROME 64
F-11 @ 1/125

Facing the Tred Avon River,
Oxford's Strand is a row of
charming waterfront homes
with stunning river views.

△ Hooper Straight Lighthouse

SHEILA H. PARKER
NIKON 6006
KODAK 200
F-16

The 1879 "screwpile" lighthouse is one of only three surviving on the Bay. It was restored and relocated to the Maritime Museum at Navy Point from Hooper Strait 39 miles South of St. Michaels in 1967.

▷ Lady Freedom

ALLISON MORRIS
CANON A-1
FUJI -100
F-11 @ 1/60

A marvelous piece of folk art, Lady Freedom was actually too heavy to mount on a ship. Until the United States Navel Academy donated her to the Chesapeake Bay Maritime Museum, she sat on the grounds at Annapolis serving as a good luck talisman for midshipmen needing a little help with their grades.

Sculpted

CHARLES PRAHL
CONTAX ST
KODACHROME 64
1/500

On this blustery cold day at
Cambridge's Great Marsh Park, the
salty spray appears to freeze in
midair over the crusted pilings.

Elegant Beauty

COURTESY OF
DAVID BISHOP
NIKON N -905
KODACHROME 64
F-8 @ 1/125

The historic Bullitt House shares a
corner with Easton's commodious
Tidewater Inn and it's theatrical
gem, the Avalon Theater.

◁ **Talbot County Courthouse, c.1794**

COURTESY OF
DAVID BISHOP
NIKON 8008
KODACHROME 200
F-11 @ 1/125

Easton became the county seat in 1788, but court records for the county date to 1662 when court was held in justices' private homes. Talbot boasts more shoreline than any other county in the continental US. It would take quite some time to thoroughly explore both its history and its shoreline!

△ **Landmark Inn** *(top)*

DR. CARL F. HAWVER
CANON AE-1
KODACHROME ELITE
AUTO

Robert Morris was known as the financier of the American Revolution. The Inn was built in 1710 overlooking the Tred Avon River from Oxford. James A. Michener, author of "Chesapeake" rated the crab cakes served here highest of any restaurant on the Eastern Shore.

△ **Courthouse Row, Easton** *(bottom)*

COURTESY OF
DAVID BISHOP
NIKON F 4
KODACHROME 200
F-56 @ 1/60

Easton is proud to have been rated 8th in the book, *The 100 Best Small Towns in America.* Its downtown features independent merchants and locally owned eateries.

Keyhole

STUART M. JOHNSON
NIKON N80
FUJI HQ 100
F-11

A moonlit streetscape beckons at the other end of an arched brick walkway in Easton.

Firefighters at Work

GLORIA FAULKNER
NIKON N 70
KODAK 400

Volunteer firemen are a crucial part of life on the Shore. Their heroism in saving the historic structure that housed the town's only toy store was poignant for Eastonians.

Early Start

CHARLES PRAHL
CONTAX ST
KODACHROME 64
1/125

An oyster tonger's workday begins before dawn at Choptank Bridge, Cambridge. The process of harvesting the oysters with long hand tongs has remained the same for over a century, but the catch is greatly reduced due to environmental pressures.

Sunset At Blackwater

D. GRAHAM SLAUGHTER
HASSABLAD
NPS
F-4.5

Patterns of migratory birds line the
red hued sky, while the tide ebbs on
another magnificent day at Blackwater National Wildlife Refuge.

△ **Hoist or Furl?**

COURTESY OF
DAVID H. STEVENS
GRAPHLEX 4XS
TMAX 100
F-22

The set of a working skipjack's sail is adjusted to make ready for the work of oyster spatting. Bay watermen are independent operators in a rugged life, making ends meet without big company benefits or corporate subsidy.

▷ **Spatting**

COURTESY OF
DAVID H. STEVENS
CANON EOS
TMAX 100
F-13

With recent declines in the oyster stocks, skipjacks find work spatting for the state. Spatting involves dumping hatchery-raised seed oysters or "spat" back onto natural oyster bars to replenish the depleted fishery.

△ **Marsh at Blackwater**

CHARLES PRAHL
CONTAX ST
KODACHROME 64
1/250

Tidal wetlands are the filters of the estuarine ecosystem, removing excess nutrients from the water, stabilizing the shoreline, and providing habitat to a plethora of creatures. Salt marshes are formed when "Spartina" or cord grasses establish a foothold in the underlying peat.

▷ **Nesting** *(top)*

CHARLES PRAHL
CONTAX ST
KODACHROME 64
1/250

Finding a nesting site is serious business. It must be in open land with good visibility, but able to withstand ice, wind and be dry in high water. But it shouldn't be on dry land either, as predators get an advantage. A marshy island is perfect.

▷ **Patriotic Bird** *(bottom)*

CHARLES PRAHL
CONTAX ST
KODACHROME 64
1/250

A vigilant bald eagle, photographed at Blackwater Nation Wildlife Refuge, which has one of the largest populations of nesting bald eagles on the Atlantic Coast.

△ **St. Michaels Aloft**

COURTESY OF
HUNTER H. HARRIS
PENTEX SF 10
FUJI 200
F-8 1000/SEC.

▷ **Canoeing on the Choptank
near Denton**

COURTESY OF
DAVID H. STEVENS
CANON EOS
KODACHROME
F-8

△ **Church near Denton**

COURTESY OF
DAVID H. STEVENS
CANON EOS
KODACHROME
F-11

The vestibule gracefully follows the gable pitch lines. Traditional red doors symbolize safety and sanctity within.

▷ **Enchanted Landscape**

GLORIA FAULKNER
NIKON N 70
KODAK ROYAL GOLD
F-5.6

Blackwater National Wildlife Refuge covers more than 20,000 acres of spectacular wetlands habitat. While people come here to hike, bike, fish, crab, hunt, or watch birds, for many it is a place of and for reflection.

△ **Ready to Sail**

CHARLES PRAHL
CONTAX ST
KODACHROME 64
1/125

Working skipjack *Howard*, built in 1909, is
ready to sail to local oyster beds and dredge
for the catch while under canvas.

▷ **Tonger on Choptank River** *(top)*

CHARLES PRAHL
CONTAX ST
KODACHROME 64
1/250

Tonging for oysters by hand is a tough and
noble way to make a living.

▷ **Measuring Up** *(bottom)*

CHARLES PRAHL
CONTAX ST
KODACHROME 64
1/125

Waterman and recreational crabbers must cull their
crab catch and throw back the undersized. Legal
limits are 5 inches from tip to tip for "jimmies" or
males, 3 inches for peelers and 3.5 inches for soft
crabs. No size limits are set for mature females or
"sooks," but wisdom dictates leaving them to
spawn for the next year's harvest.

Wash Day

TERRANCE H. VACHA
NIKON CP 950
1600X1200 DIGITAL
F-9.9 @ 1/89

A Knapps Narrows waterman
cleans crab pots.

Fishy Business

TERRANCE H. VACHA
NIKON CP 950
1600X1200 DIGITAL
F-3.6 @ 1/793

A pair of waterman sort their catch
after a haul.

Decomposition

ERIN K. FLUHARTY
PENTAX 160
400

A derelict boat at Knapps Narrows turns
bewitching photographic fodder as the tide
rises. Disappearing gunwales and blistering
paint reveal only mystery and questions.

△ **Solitary**

DAVID A. BENHOFF
PENTAX 645
FUJI NPH 400

An old skiff grounded in the marsh takes the sun.

▷ **Ready Transport**

DAVID A. BENHOFF
PENTAX 645

Two skiffs in the foreground and two crab boats behind - ready to convey their crews to favorite crabbing grounds.

On the Railway

ALBERT WARFEL
CANON DIGITAL 5100
AUTO

An old workhorse languishes on its
backyard railway awaiting some
refurbishment. Imagine the stories
this boat could tell from years of
working on the water in every kind
of weather.

Strapped In

TERRANCE H. VACHA
NIKON CP 950
1600X1200 DIGITAL
F-6.8 @ 1/505

Southern Cross is suspended from a travelift for a hauling & cleaning at Knapps Narrows.

The Drawbridge Is Up

HUNTER H. HARRIS
ALOFT AERIAL PHOTOGRAPHY
NIKON 8008
FUJI 200
8/1000/SEC.

Separating Tilghman Island from the mainland, Knapps Narrows is the gateway to yachting, sport fishing and all the charms of this working waterman's village. The old counter-balanced drawbridge from 1932 is now the entranceway to the Chesapeake Bay Maritime Museum.

Three Masted Ship at Navy Point

HUNTER H. HARRIS
ALOFT AERIAL PHOTOGRAPHY
PENTAX SF 10
FUJI 200
8/1000/SEC.

Take a bird's eye view of the Chesapeake Bay Maritime Museum with the famous Crab Claw restaurant at lower left. An excursion boat is moored next to the Crab Claw. Hooper Strait lighthouse is to the right.

Blackwater Classic

D. GRAHAM SLAUGHTER
F5 NIKON
PRO COLOR
F-5.6

More than 250 species of birds are
regularly seen throughout the year
at Blackwater. Most are migratory,
so it pays to visit at least quarterly
to enjoy the full diversity.

△ **The Inn at Easton, Circa 1790**

ALLISON MORRIS
CANON A-1
FUJI -100
F-16 @ 1/60

An elegant Federal mansion is now home to a luxury inn and world-class restaurant.

◁ **The Bridge to Nowhere**

MARY GALLO
PENTAX ZOOM 60X
35 MM

Crab pots at Hoopers Island are stacked high and ready for the crabs to start running.

In The Sticks

STEPHANIE KUHN
1955 CANON
KODAK 400
F-11

One tumbleweed cloud appears ready
to bounce across the tops of ancient
treetops in the Blackwater marsh. The
still water of the tidal wetland records
it all.

△ **Early Morning Trot Liner**

HONORABLE MENTION

CHARLES PRAHL
CONTAX ST
KODACHROME 200
1/125

A Choptank River waterman works
his lines. The hours are long and
the work is tough but certain pay-
offs—like this sunrise—are hard to
assign a value.

▷ **Up the Creek**

MICHAEL J. KABLER
CANON A-1
FUJI -100
F-5.6 @ 1/60

An old buy boat patiently waits for
a change in circumstances.

Postcard

STEPHANIE LATHAM
MINOLTA 500 DI

A stately relic is almost returned to
its former glory by the last rays of
an early fall day. Three distinct eras
are represented on the grounds of
this former manor house on Rt. 50
outside Easton.

Steam Powered

MARY HITCHENS
CANON EOS ELANII
KODAK PORTRA NC
F-8

Wilbur, Ritchie and Timmy Engle
pose with the recently restored
Frick Steamer, which ran the
sawmill.

If Vermeer Had Camera...

MARY HITCHENS
CANON EOS ELANII
KODAK PORTRA NC
F-8

Harvested wheat awaiting the
threshing machine at Tuckahoe
Steam and Gas Show in Talbot
County.

Thrashing the Wheat

MARY HITCHENS
CANON EOS ELANII
KODAK PORTRA NC
F-5.6

Timmy Engle feeds the wheat-
thrashing machine at the Tuckahoe
Steam and Gas Show. The annual
show provides a rare opportunity
to experience the agricultural her-
itage of the region.

Living History

MARY HITCHENS
CANON EOS ELANII
KODAK PORTRA NC
F-6.7

A collaborative camera and a vintage wheat thrashing operation in full swing bring the past to life.

Roadside Bounty *(top)*

CHRISTINA N. GRANBERG
CANON EOS REBEL X
KODAK GOLD 400
F -5.6

Mouthwateringly fresh produce is sold all over the shore from roadside stands in season. Haggling over the price of melons, peaches, corn and strawberries is part of Eastern Shore culture. The vidalia onions, of course, are "not from around here."

Family Farm *(bottom)*

JILL E. YOUSE
CANON REBEL
200
F-8

21-month-old Patrick Youse loves to feed the cows and help his Daddy on the tractor at their Ridgely farm.

Glorious Morning

SHERILL HERBERT
KODAK
KODAK 200 GOLD
AUTO

The Choptank River Bridge at sunrise from Great Marsh Park. A flock of Canada geese floats in foreground.

Talbot County Idyll

STUART M. JOHNSON
NIKON F 100
FUJI HQ 100
F-8

Surprisingly large boats retire in the
shoal water at the head of a creek,
accessible only by canoe or dinghy.

Third Haven Friends Meeting

ALLISON MORRIS
CANON A-1
FUJI -100
F-16 @ 1/125

Completed in 1684, Third Haven is one of the state's most important historic structures. Of national note, it is the oldest frame house of worship in continuous, available use in the United States. Visitors today will find the same spirit of mindful silence as did William Penn and other notables who visited and worshipped here over 300 years ago.

△ Backroads Barn

LISA COLEMAN
OLYMPUS 35 MM

Layers of light and paint reveal some of the history of this old barn at Goldsborough Neck. It harkens back to a day when wide wood planks from nearby stands of timber were used to construct agricultural buildings.

◁ Oxford-Bellevue Ferry

MARY HITCHENS
CANON EOS ELANII
KODAK PORTRA NC
F-16

A romantic getaway weekend in Oxford begins with an arrival by ferry. Established in 1683, the Oxford-Bellevue ferry is believed to be the nation's oldest privately operated ferry service.

Working Families

HEATHER BROWN
FUJI
800 SPEED

Heather Brown shot this photograph
of Buffalo Strong and his son Jamie of
Reprisal marking their catfish pots
while she and her husband fished
their nets near them on the Choptank
near Denton.

Lower Shore

The Road to Deal (*previous page*)

COURTESY OF
RICHARD FORD
NIKON
200

Central by water but remote by
land, Deal Island's geography made
it the center of oyster harvesting
many years ago. With oyster harvests a fraction of what they once
were, Deal Island has become a
sleepy backwater with a 13,000-
acre wildlife management area.
Explore the trails and don't miss the
annual Labor Day Skipjack Races.

△ **The Beach on Deal Island**

JOSHUA STEVEN BREWER
NIKON F-5
KODAK 400

But for the clouds, time stands still
on the unspoiled shores of Deal
Island on Tangier Sound. Feel the
fresh breeze off the Bay at the public beach.

▷ **Maryland Moment**

CAROLYN SCHWEIKERT
CANON EOS ELAN
KODAK 200
AUTO

One of the dwindling fleet of Deal
Island skipjacks, this captain gives
an excursion sail to help with the
upkeep of his boat. Many of the
boats have been added to the
National Register as distinctive historic craft.

That's What I'm Talking About! *(top)*

SHEILA H. PARKER
NIKON 6006
KODAK 200
F-5.6

It just doesn't get any better than when that long awaited first crab of the season just happens to be a big, fat whale.

Crab Derby *(bottom)*

COURTESY OF
DAVID BISHOP
NIKON F4S
KODACHROME 64
F-4 @ 1/250

Perhaps not yet rivaling the Kentucky Derby, but in Crisfield, where crab is king, this is serious sport! Crabs come from as far away as Hawaii to compete.

Old Becomes New

HONORABLE MENTION

TERRANCE H. VACHA
NIKON CP 950
1600X1200 DIGITAL
F-6.0 @ 1/61

In the changing waterfront at Crisfield, tourism and industry exist side by side. Terry Vacha and his wife spent a few weeks last summer cruising the Chesapeake Bay on their 26' sailboat *Tranquility*. Terry is an Associate Professor of Physics and his wife teaches high school students with special needs. As visitors from Cleveland, Ohio who love photography, sailing, and wildlife they have a unique perspective on the area. They enjoy the slower pace of life, and the friendliness of the residents. Being prospective retirees to the area who are experienced in sailing other regions, they are charmed with the quaint towns, seaports and scores of anchorages but note that all stakeholders who use the Bay need to do much more to protect the fragile marine environment.

Making Tracks

JOANNE C. GADOMSKI
MINOLTA 5XI
KODAK GOLD 100-6
F-5.6

Legend has it that the ancestors of today's wild pony population at Assateague Island were survivors of a 16th century Spanish ship which foundered in a storm. This little one is the youngest of a small but sturdy herd that thrives on the island today.

Public Landing, Maryland

STEPHANIE EWELL
CANON 35 MM

The plain name belies the stunning views from this tiny enclave on Chincoteague Bay. A crabbing boat is docked on the sheltered inlet that was once homeport for numerous boats working the area. Birders will find pelicans here.

Dune Afternoon

JOANNE C. GADOMSKI
MINOLTA 5XI
KODAK GOLD 100-6
F-5.6

Ocean City occupies one of the barrier islands—one of those slender sandy spits of land that bear the brunt of wind and weather all year, but provide recreational havens for vacationers in season.

△ **The Seasons Change**

LINDA RIGGIN
MINOLTA MAXXIM 7000
FUJICOLOR

Summer rounds the bend to find
fall color at secluded Whitehaven,
looking across the Wicomico River
to Somerset County.

◁ **18th Century Gem**

ALLISON MORRIS
CANON A-1
FUJI 100
F-16 @ 1/60

A classic telescope cottage, "The
Little House" is now part of the
Riverside Inn Bed and Breakfast in
Snow Hill.

△ The Old Lime Plant

HARVEY D. TYLER
VIVATAR 35 MM
400

Standing quietly vigilant over Crisfield's waterfront, this abandoned sentinel is a monument to previous generations of industry.

▷ Barging Up the Nanticoke

SANDY ATKINSON
KODAK ONE TIME USE
REG I PANORAMIC

A load of stone makes its way past Sharptown. Despite the industrial shift from rivers to roads, waterways still provide the most economical transport for many bulk products.

Long Gone Cedar

MARK ANDREW TYLER
VIVATAR 35 MM
400

A weatherworn stump is a solitary
reminder of a forest that once
stood in what is now Janes Island
State Park, near Crisfield.

Silvery Hammock

HARVEY D. TYLER
VIVATAR 35 MM
400

A hammock at the shoreline where
Broad Creek empties into the Little
Annemessex River bears the effects

Composition

ALAN C. DICKERSON
MINOLTA 330 SI
100

Mt. Pleasant United Methodist Church
in Willards serves a Wicomico County
municipality with population less than
1,000 as well as the surrounding rural
community. In addition to the church-
yard cemeteries, Eastern Shore counties
each have dozens of family graveyards.

Belltower at Salisbury University

JODI LYNN HUDSON
NIKON N80
KODAK EKTECHROME 100
F-16

Salisbury University serves more than
6,000 students. Through its impressive
outreach program, it is also the heart
of the larger shore community. The
belltower has always carried a special
significance for Jodi Hudson, who
grew up across the street and now
attends the school.

Feeding the Gulls

CHARLES PRAHL
CONTAX ST
KODACHROME 64
1/125

The ratio of gulls to humans shifts
in summer when city folk flock
"downy ocean" to Ocean City.
Otherwise rural, Worcester
County includes Maryland's major
Atlantic beach resort.

Sunset Looking Glass

KAREN COATES
NIKON F2
VELVIA
F-16 24MM LENS

Water and sky find common
ground where they join at the
marsh and forest.

Where the Fun Never Sets

JOSHUA STEVEN BREWER
NIKON F-5
FUJI 200

Ocean City nightlife goes on and on, round and round.

Sunset Silhouette

JOSHUA STEVEN BREWER
NIKON F-5
KODAKMAX 400

The sun retreats into the western bay, signaling last call for a day of shelling at Deal Island.

Berry Picking

ANDREW B. RUSNAK
PENTAX SF1
FUJI
F-11

A very young strawberry picker harvests some of the shore's sweet-
est bounty. Local berries are smaller, redder and sweeter than West
Coast fare. Picked ripe, they're celebrated at strawberry festivals all
over the shore during the first two weeks of June.

High and Dry

ERNEST W. PICK
NIKON
VELVIA
F-16

Awaiting the next tide to venture
forth in search of the blue crab.

Commodious Home (top)

ALLISON MORRIS
CANON A-1
FUJI 100
F-16@ 1/125

A 19th century residence recalls a time when Poco-moke City was one of the truck farming capitols of the United States.

Solitary Fishing Shack, Smith Island (bottom)

ELIZABETH CONSTANTINI
MINOLTA 800 SI
KODAK GOLD 200

The isolated communities that occupy Smith Island, reached by boat from Crisfield, are some of the last bastions of a culture that has all but disappeared. Smith Islanders, like their Virginia counterparts on Tangier Island to the south, are completely dependent on the Chesapeake Bay, which surrounds them. They have a unique dialect, which traces directly to the Elizabethan English of their forbearers.

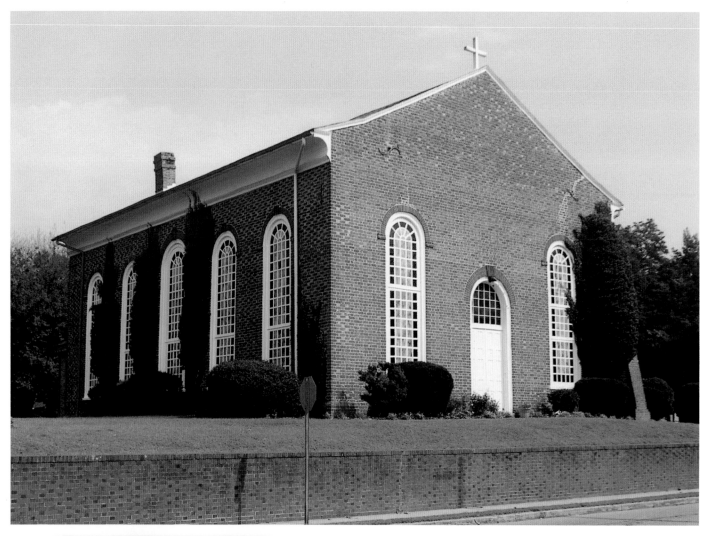

△ Steeped in History

ALLISON MORRIS
CANON A-1
FUJI 100
F-16@ 1/125

The Anglican congregation established All Hallows in 1692. The present Episcopal church was completed in 1756, with modifications in 1872 and 1899. The bricks are believed to have arrived from England as ships' ballast. A bible and bell given to the community by Queen Anne are here, as well as a treasure trove of genealogical information in the surrounding cemetery.

◁ All Hallows Episcopal Church

ALLISON MORRIS
CANON A-1
FUJI 100
F-16@ 1/125

This lovely historic church in Snow Hill is notable for its Flemish bond construction, beautiful windows, and carefully groomed, small leaved Kenilworth Ivy.

Worcester County Courthouse, Snow Hill

ALLISON MORRIS
CANON A-1
FUJI 100
F-11@ 1/125

Snow Hill was settled by the second generation of colonists out of Jamestown, Virginia at
the navigational head of the Pocomoke River.
It became a royal port and shipbuilding center.
The current courthouse dates to 1894 in a
county bounded by both the scenic river
and the mighty Atlantic Ocean.

The Globe Theater

ALLISON MORRIS
CANON A-1
FUJI 100
F-8 @ 1/60

In the lee of Ocean City, revitalized Berlin (pronounced Burl'in) has a Victorian downtown not to be missed. The Globe is the arts center for a town that has been the set for an Anne Tyler novel and two feature films—Runaway Bride and Tuck Everlasting.

Pocomoke River Canoe Company

ALLISON MORRIS
CANON A-1
FUJI 100
F-11@ 1/125

Explore the Pocomoke's scenic upper reaches from this outfitter in Snow Hill. You will find the northernmost range of bald cypress in a unique environment and see firsthand the endless variety of the Eastern Shore.

▷ Makemie Memorial Presbyterian Church

ALLISON MORRIS
CANON A-1
FUJI 100
F-16 @ 1/60

Snow Hill's Presbyterian church is the first of the American denomination, originally established in 1683 by Francis Makemie. The present structure in the Gothic Revival style dates to 1889.

A Tale of Two Bridges

COURTESY OF
RICHARD FORD
NIKON
200

The old bridge goes into Pocomoke
City and the new bridge bypasses
it. From his Ercoupe cockpit, Dick
Ford illustrates the relationship of
the town to the deep winding river.

Princess Anne

COURTESY OF
RICHARD FORD
NIKON
200

The county seat of Somerset is
the home of the University of
Maryland, Eastern Shore and a
priceless treasure trove of architectural gems and regional lore.

Storm Brewing

MARK ANDREW TYLER
VIVATAR 35 MM
400

Weather builds up fast and unpre-
dictably on the open waters of the
Chesapeake Bay. This storm is at
Great Point, Tangier Sound.

Shore Life

FAUNA, FLORA, AND ACTIVITIES

State Flower (previous page)

ELIZABETH CONSTANTINI
MINOLTA 800 SI
KODAK GOLD 200

Maryland's state flower, the black-
eyed Susan, makes its aesthetic
statement in a small town garden.

△ ## Visitors From Canada

STUART M. JOHNSON
NIKON N 80
KODAK 400 T-MAX
F-4.5

Canada Geese react to the photographer's intrusion by bursting into
the air. They'll soon be back to
resume their gleaning of the corn-
field stubble, which feeds thousands
of these visitors from their arrival in
the fall until their departure which
heralds the arrival of spring.

Pensive

JOANNE C. GADOMSKI
MINOLTA XG -1
KODAK GOLD 100-6
F-4

A solitary gull stands at surf's edge,
sunrise.

What Are You Looking At?

CYNTHIA PILCHARD
CANON AE1
35MM

Sea gulls outnumber humans in
much of Worcester County.

Blue Crab

LINDA LITTLEFIELD
MINOLTA
FUJICA 400

The Eastern Shore's principal mascot and the mainstay of its seafood industry, the handsome "jimmie" here is caught by the hind paddle. Callinectes sapidus, the noble blue crab's scientific name, translates to "savory beautiful swimmers."

Looking for Lunch

EMERSON M. TODD, JR.
SAMSUNG 140
KODAK 800 SPEED

An egret pair patiently waits for
lunch to swim within range in one
of the bountiful creeks of lower
Dorchester County.

Who's More Surprised?

LINDA C. RIGGIN
MINOLTA MAXIM 7000
FUJICOLOR

A baby opossum surprised the
photographer in Wicomico County.
Or was it the reverse? The Eastern
Shore's resident marsupial can be
found everywhere.

What's for Dinner?

AMANDA J. BENCHOFF
PENTAX IQZOOM EC4
35MM

Cookie voices her opinion on pasture politics or possibly the local cuisine in rural Caroline County.

Pink Dogwood Blossom

R. WAYNE KNOWLES
MINOLTA
KODAK GOLD
F-3.5

This colorful harbinger of spring, caught in a split second to enjoy year round.

Green Peace

R. WAYNE KNOWLES
MINOLTA
KODAK GOLD
F-5.0

A variegated fritillary aflight in a
verdant summer garden.

All Seeing Osprey

TERRANCE H. VACHA
NIKON CP 950
1600X1200 DIGITAL
F-6.6 @ 1/215

Ospreys defend their nests, often on channel markers in creeks or rivers, until their young can fly off and fend for themselves.

Swans at Dusk

MARGE DEDERBECK
CANON EOS 10
KODAK
F-5.6

Sharing parental duties, mute swans vigorously defend their territory until the cygnets can stake out their own area. In fact, the mute swan will aggressively hiss if its mate or cygnets are threatened.

Three's Company

TERRANCE H. VACHA
NIKON CP 950
1600X1200 DIGITAL

Three snowy egrets at rest on
Assateague Island. When the tide
changes, the fishing will improve.

◁ **Aromatic**

CYNTHIA PILCHARD
CANON AE1
35MM

A swallowtail butterfly investigates a lilac bush.

△ **Anticipation**

DAVID A. BENHOFF
PENTAX 645

A field of sunflowers eagerly greets the day.

Sandy Atkinson
24900 Riverton Cut-Off Road
Mardela Springs, MD 21837
sandytwink@aol.com
97

Richard Taylor Bailey
5551 Quaker Neck Landing
Road
Chestertown, MD 21620
qnlmd@toad.net
21, 24–25, 26–27

Amanda J. Benchoff
1126 Camp Road
Denton, MD 21629
122

David A. Benhoff
PO Box 65
Secretary, MD 21664
benhoff@intercom.net
69(2), 127

Dave Bishop
35 E. Dover Street
Easton, MD 21601
competitionphoto@yahoo.com
46, 49, 50, 51, 92

Virginia Breuninger
204 Waldo Drive
Chestertown, MD 21620
breuning@intercom.net
15

Joshua Steven Brewer
30507 Danwood Drive
Delmar, MD 21875
brewer@shore.intercom.net
1, 90, 104(2)

Heather Brown
9555 Fisher Road
Denton, MD 21629
15, 87

Mary Bryan
106 Tred Avon Avenue
Easton, MD 21601
wilder101@hotmail.com
27

Karen Coates
10401 Grosvenor Place, # 515
Rockville, MD 20852
karcoat@yahoo.com
3, 102–103

Lisa Coleman
6 South Street, Apt C
Easton, MD 21601
lisaanncoleman@hotmail.com
86

Elizabeth Constantini
549 Princeton Court
Bensalem, PA 19020
107, 114–115

Marge Dederbeck
6753 Holly Woods Road
Sherwood, MD 21665
theruz1@aol.com
124

Alan C. Dickerson
5053 Airport Road
Salisbury, MD, 21804
acd1234@netzero.net
back cover, 1, 100

Norman C. Dulak
22950 Fairgale Farm Lane
Chestertown, MD 21620
ndulak@crosslink.com
9, 16, 30

James R. Durham III
132 Blue Note Farm Lane
Church Hill, MD 21623
jrdurham@intercom.net
31

Stacey Embert
401 Mason Branch Lane
Queen Anne, MD 21657
4, 17, 29

Stephanie Ewell
PO Box 437
Millsboro, DE 19966
lewell@ce.net
95

Gloria Faulkner
1070 N Washington Street,
Apt 202
Easton, MD 21601
glof@goeaston.net
42, 52, 62–63

Erin K. Fluharty
21609 Camper Circle
Tilghman, MD 21671
68

Richard Ford
P.O. Box 221
Upper Fairmount, MD 21867
88–89, 112(2)

Joanne C. Gadomski
24 Pequot Street
New Britain, CT 06053
vbeachjo21@aol.com
back cover, 2, 94, 95, 117

Mary Gallo
103 Buena Vista Avenue
Cambridge, MD 21613
74

Christina N. Granberg
300 Washington Avenue
Chestertown, MD 21620
christina.granberg@washcoll.edu
12, 82

Hunter H. Harris
Aloft Inc. Aerial Photography
P.O. Box 2398
Easton, MD 21601
hhh@friend.ly.net
*2, 10, 11, 26, 31, 32–33,
34, 44, 60, 72(2)*

Dr. Carl F. Hawver
3463 S. Leisure World Blvd.
Silver Spring, MD 20906-1767
CFHawver@aol.com
51

Sherill Herbert
101 Willis Street
Cambridge, MD 21613
herbert@shorenet.net
83

Mary Hitchens
1227 Raughley Hill Road
Harrington, DE 19952
8, 35, 45, 79, 80(2), 81, 86

Jodi Lynn Hudson
705 E. East Street
Delmar, MD 21875
photography7@aol.com
101

Stuart M. Johnson
16 S. Aurora Street
Easton, MD 21601
40, 44, 52, 84, 116

Michael J. Kabler
702 South Street
Easton, MD 21601
41, 43, 77

R. Wayne Knowles
3779 Rumsey Drive
Trappe, MD 21673
122, 123

Stephanie Kuhn
1511 Crocheron Road
Bishops Head, MD 21672
alhfarm@fastol.com
75

Stephanie Latham
29595-802 Dutchman's Lane
Easton, MD 21601
shutterbug@crosslink.net
5, 78–79

Linda Littlefield
PO Box 952
27047 Presquile Road
Easton, MD 21601
4, 119

Allison Morris
346 Montford Avenue, Apt 1
Asheville, NC 28801
*20–21, 24, 47, 74, 85, 96,
107, 108(2), 109, 110(2), 111*

Robert F. O'Brien
20 Brace Road
Cherry Hill, NJ 08034
robrian@tomarlaw.com
28–29

Barbara F. O'Conner
122 Bayview
Grasonville, MD 21638
16

Sheila H. Parker
242 Hill Road
Honey Brook, PA 19344
shwal@yahoo.com
5, 47, 92

Joyce M. Phillips
27 Jackson Avenue
Round Hill, VA 20141
joyphill@aol.com
41

Ernest W. Pick
4201 Bonita Avenue
Coconut Grove, FL 33133
106

Cynthia Pilchard
117 West Martin Street
Snow Hill, MD 21863
CEPilchard@aol.com
118, 126

Charles Prahl
8 Nanticoke Road
Cambridge, MD 21613
cprahl@shorenet.net
*front cover, 2, 5, 7, 18, 48, 53,
58, 59(2), 64, 65(2), 76, 102*

Linda C. Riggin
29919 Foskey Lane
Delmar, MD 21875
96, 121

Andrew B. Rusnak
7848 Shore Drive
Preston, MD 21655
105

George W. Schultz
8480 Broad Neck Road
Chestertown, MD 21620
gws@dmv.com
23

Carolyn Schweikert
407 South Kaywood Drive
Salisbury, MD 21804
clswjs@aol.com
91

D. Graham Slaughter
18318 Brickstore Road
Hamptstead, MD 21074
back cover, 1, 36, 37, 54–55, 73

David H. Stevens
609 South Street
Easton, MD 21601
dstevens@goeaston.net
19, 38, 39, 56, 57, 61, 62

Emerson M.Todd, Jr.
2548 Toddville Road
Toddville, MD 21672
120–121

Mark Andrew Tyler
3129 Stockton Road
Pocomoke, MD 21851
matyle@wm.edu
98, 113

Harvey D. Tyler
3129 Stockton Road
Pocomoke, MD 21851
97, 99

Terrance H. Vacha
128 Briarleigh Drive
Brunswick, OH 44212
tvacha@yahoo.com
66, 67, 71, 92–93, 124, 125

Robert Austin Walmsley
710 Rosen Drive
Chestertown, MD 21620
13, 14, 22

Albert Warfel
PO Box 1258
St. Michaels, MD 21663
aew@dmv.com
70

Jill E. Youse
14250 Oakland Road
Ridgely, MD 21660
youse@dmv.com
82